GUMBO TALK

NEO-SURREALIST POEMS

RONNIE MCGRATH

To Beth [illegible]
one love
Ronnie x

ankhademia press

Copyright

First published in 2010 by ankhademia press.
Ankhademia press PO Box 50034 London SE6 3WW
info@ankhademia.com

Designed by iclickdesign
sales@iclickdesign.com

A CIP catalogue reference for this book is available from the British Library.
ISBN 978-0-9549342-1-7

www.ronniemcgrath.com

Acknowledgement

For Pinky

Spiritual Blessings to -

Daisy, Lulu, Mali and Kimeya
Donovan & Lauren
Janie & Nick

...Ah Um

Charles Mingus

Contents

Becomе. ~~b-kuhm~~

Enter. BORN ♥. born into this. Change this. *CLIMB*. Achieve Δ Gain respect. Gain visibility. Gain self respect. Love self. GROW $(x+a)^n = \sum_{k=0}^{n} \binom{n}{k} x^k a^{n-k}$. Become LARGER than life®. aim HIGH. Aim over and above this ~~thiz~~. Create. Develop. Transgress. Become you. UUUU. Become a genius $\frac{-b \pm \sqrt{b^2-4ac}}{2a}$. Become omniscient £€. Become male ☻ ☺. Become female. Become life ☥ Breathe. Become energy. Live. Step into the visibility. Into the light 𓂀 Recognise yourself ☻ ☻. RISEΔ. RISE above and below. Get UP! Get UP from down! Get up from the ground. Get with it! Get knowledge! Get a hold of yourself. Get life. Get ready. Become. ~~B-KUM. B-Cuhm~~. Born into this. Change this. CLIMB. Reach for the sky. *FFFFFFFFF* FLY.

Diasfrican(s)

I put myself on the line and might never be published/might never be liked/might never be needed/my poetry wild as innovation/lights ablaze with language/reservoirs of some radical speech act/ emotions running high/rich in haiku-globin/in and out of form/jouissance/buck wild and naked poetry art/untamed voice of some past etching seeping through my verse/alphabetically coded fridge magnets waking me from sleep/ from psychotherapy/from costume dramas of Freudian dream tablets/scopophilic movie houses/spray painting rooms with manifestos of dada-glyphics / manifestos of hierarchical-glyphics/the spectacle of spectacle poems looking back on Sankofa birds/the past of our present findings/trapped here/in a culture of wires and technology/tuning me in/dropping me out/tuning me in/dropping me out/my eyes of computer screens/a virtual surface noise in saliva and steel/tattooed body armour/expressionist fish scale/broken off/ severed/amputated/i am closed/hermetically sealed/persona non-grata/ fucked/putting myself on the line/a textile pattern in fluorescent daybreak/ writing in some Jackson Pollock rendition of serendipity/scratched upon flesh of palimpsest scars/superimposed ancient graffiti paintwork/older than cobwebs/than lime scale/than numerals/than times infinity/than repetition/the tattooed language of needle tongues/the knife-sharp language of expletives/like the speed driven bodies of crashed cars/swollen vehicles/ beaten into submission/beaten into pan/beaten into calypso and rhythm/ sparrows news item mightier than a sword/a weh di man wid de hammer go?/tell me/a weh di man wi di hammer go?/Nubian cyborgs of my peoples language in plumes of exotic affluenza/ contagious offerings to the high priestess/to the vernacular women of vernacular cultures/interneti-zens of the virtual world/carnivores of some female paradissimo/putting me on the line/my locality global/got me thinking in the general and the specific of these paradigm shifts/my linguistic furnishing/my linguistic clothes/ the hypertextualised transsexual frameworks of some rapid ear movement/ eavesdropping on rippled water/exoteric silk circles in the guise of magic/ vignetted shades of the plain and silent shapes of things to come/

Hi-koo

This/ text/ makes/ no/ sense
For lan/guage/ is/ hid/den in
A/false/im/pres/sion

Of/re/a/li/ty
Ex/is/ting/out/side/of/thought
Out/side/ of/ meaning

Gi/ven/ to/ us/ in
Sym/bols/ and/ punc/tu/ation
Scratch/ marks/ of/ process

In/ten/ded/ mean/ing
Un/der/stood/ by/ the/ many
Who/ can/ read/ the/bones

And/ know/ their/ world/ is
A/highly/me/di/a/ted
Cut/up/of/all/things

Vis/u/al/and/texts
Con/struc/ted/for/the/reel/2
Reel/of/ci/ne/ma

Mingus Music Act II

Bones and trumpet notes/water-melanin music climbing out of holes/ climbing out of pipes/beautiful airshaft of winged spirits in the company of flutes/intricate fingers of feminine slippers blown from glass/cymbals of fire infesting the drummers stick with paradiddles of rain falling on the rusty roofs of aborted shanty towns/the music begins with polemics of black nationalisms/some call it a cliché/but we all know that it is a free jazz composition purchased on credit cards/revolution for sale/long live consumerism/power to the beetle/PAUSE!/there is a silence here/there is a complicit silence here/there is a deafening silence here/can you hear it?/ the music begins with brush strokes/textures of Pablo Picasso/Beauford Delaney/and Jean-Michel Basquait/I was coloured once/pretty as a painting/ but now I speak in the postmodern tongues of urbanity/symbols of youth culture in the non-static order of contemporary language/black speech-flows colonising microphones with gumbo talk/syncretic angel feathers lost in their own dreams/rhythms of themselves simulacrumised/Bones and trumpet notes/Negropolitanarianisms/strolling through my thoughts in an iambic pentameter of unadulterated Phunk/Philosophunk/a metafictitiously wonderful head space of untreated fabulation/of fiction gone wild/poet trees shedding their autumnal leaves as the provocative landscapes of her female anatomy comes gliding through the science fiction of long tunnels/ there isn't even time to count my eye-lashes/for when the music flows/ fire turns to rainbows/prismatic screens of spectrum glass/riding the high hat in some intertextual quiltwork of calligraphy pens/scribing their maliferous etchings onto the blue notations of pure colour/servo-mechanistic forces of nano-visions giving sight to the impotent lens of blind telescopes/ micro theories of cultures in contention/macro-theories of verbose finger puppets/scarifications of deep tyre tracks rolling across the dusty roads of a new frontier/these outlines of my lips in red chilli pepper/hot woman sauce/minkisi music/how I like my jazz!!!!/ribbons of peace doves taking to the air in an ontogonous migration of neo-surrealisms/optophones of some radical improvisation/reaching light years into the circle of things/the motion of motion in the motion of songs/kickin' it in the sound waves of your paradise/enter you pulchritudinous spirits into these smoke filled rooms of beatniks and peace pipes.

The Rainbow of Her Beauty

In the celebrity of
Camera-shoots
And magazine covers

Bare breasted models
Inflate their lips with
The frantic cries of billboard messages

Thin but not quite waif enough
To dine with butterflies
The faceless strings of their hidden beauty
Sharpen scalpel-blades

As the plastic surgeon
Sturdy as a hungry penis makes an incision
And pours the wealth of stockbrokers
Into their teenage thighs

And as the secrets of their thongs
Peek out of hipster-trousers
Titillating monsters

The schoolyards of their innocent years
Throw dead skipping ropes
Into the tears of polluted riverbeds.

RONNIE

Poor [~~traitors~~ traits] of the People Act VIII

Them.Think.Me.Stupid.Me.Think.Them.Stupid.Them.Think.Me.Stupid. Me.Think.Them.Stupid.Them.Think.Me.Stupid.Me.Think.Them.Stupid. Them.Think.Me.Fool.Me.Think.Them.Fool.Them.Think.Me.Fool.Me. Think.Them.Fool.Them.Think.Me.Fool.Me.Think.Them.Fool.Them. Think. Me.Dark.Me.Think.Them.Light.Them.Think.Me.Dark.Me.Think.Them. Light.Them.Think.Me.Dark.Me.Think.Them.Light.Them.Think.Me.Gay. Me.Think.Them.Straight.Them.Think.Me.Gay.Me.Think.Them.Straight. Them.Think.Me.Gay.Me.Think.Them.Straight.Them.Think.Me.Poor. Me.Think.Them.Rich.Them.Think.Me.Poor.Me.Think.Them.Rich.Them. Think.Me.Poor.Me.Think.Them.Rich.Them.Think.Me.Male.Me.Think. Them.Female.Them.Think.Me.Male.Me.Think.Them.Female.Them.Think. Me.Male.Me.Think.Them.Female.Them.Think.Me.Evil.Me.Think.Them. Good.Them.Think.Me.Evil.Me.Think.Them.Good.Them.Think.Me.Evil. Me.Think.Them.Good.Them.Think.Me.Evil.Me.Think.Them.Good. Them.Think.Me.Believe.Me.Think.Them.Believe.Them.Think.Me.Believe. Me.Think.Them.Believe.Them.Think.Me.Believe.Me.Think.Them.Believe. Them.Think.Me.Think.Me.Think.Them.Think.Them.Think.Me.Think. Me.Think.Them.Think.

Ronnie

The Catalyst: Ode to Sun Ra

Your burst of Sun Ra is an incredible drinking water of ebony rain capsules imprinted on the sun-baked earth in a golden footfall of glorious experimentation/the future of your visions are with us now/colouring the air with renditions of the peacocks tail feathers/the ankh-like features of my black nose hip to your frankincense and hip to your myrrh/the incense smoke of your spirituality/enveloping my soul with the ineffable fingerprints of jazz compositions/communicating in polysemic voices of genre music/polysemic voices of rage/polysemic voices of peace makers/throwing splashes of minkisi medicine into the minds of abstract oil painters/the coded universe of your signs and your symbols is an intense language of no compromise/I know you would rather die alone than drown a slow death in this watered down version of reality/the straight world of conformity was never for you/ you were not seduced by the superfluous skins of their fashion houses/and unlike the so-called revolutionaries of this artistry/you did not even succumb to the scent of their bank notes/that green obsession of man-made isms/ capitalisms food mountains stacked like burger piles of cash/hamburgers of obesities screening off like the Hollywood effect of a hit movie in this primitive world of logo-centrism/ritualistic earth practice of bizarre hierarchies/mannequins of oppression/taxonomising children with the jewels of their clothes/sexualised garments of intricate lace patterns/black lace colourings cooler than negritude/black lace colourings of exoticism/black lace colourings of mobile telephone masts/pirating the airwaves/subverting culture with a push towards the new frontiers of futuristic travellers on their way to Sun Ra country/the DNA of avante-guardism/where theory meets practice and practice makes perfection out of your finest art/ark-works of Noah's crossing into the sublime landscapes of a new music hidden in an eyeball/the stuff of light bulbs emanating from the keys with smooth sound textures tasting like skin blisters when set down upon the stones of tongues/ tongue textures feeling like a woman in slow motion/feeling like a woman in song/her voice/bouncing off the wall/exploding in my ear like the secret language of a whisper/I offer her a butterfly and still she smears my lips with the herstories of a womanist fiction/heterodiegetic narratives of the pharaohs coming/premonitions of black star liners shaping out of the sky like the indelible mark of a comet/shaping out of the sky like an ankh/ pyramids of geometric sand dunes sticking out of the desert in the breast-like features of thorns/she beckons me to mine this African flesh of a rich mineral earth/subcutaneous rivers of invention forcing eczema to appear on the outer frames of mountain bikes/the intensity of your music is just one of the roads which I have walked to meet her here/she a treasure trove of stanza patterns/she the automatic writing of my soul inscribed upon a wish to be free in life and in art/she much more than just some empty play of words/ she an ode to you Sun Ra/myth maker and master of invention/the catalyst/ he who changes everything but forever stays the same/

Ronnie

Solitary Focks Scene I

~~OUT SOURCED OUT FOks~~ FOX

Solitary fox/lonely as a planet/you/pushed into the prison house of property and ownership/these streets are mean/much meaner than Soweto's cardboard cities/much meaner than deflated pension schemes/mean streets must mean something/something must mean/must count/count we must for something other than tarmac/concrete/and/the unique sameness of ~~ladyfication~~ gentrification/solitary fox your habitat/pulled from under your feet like a rug/environment ~~beaten eaten~~ devoured/by the voracious mouths of expansionism/nowhere to run/nowhere to sun/in this onslaught of a perverse makeover/in this over-imaginative game of frontierism/my mother nature wounded/muscle bound/obese/stuck in her ways like the alienated language of colloquial fridge magnets/quantified and inebriated/I come in from the cold and contemplate the digital high of philosophical page numbers/and old Mr fox is as cunning as a rabbit/the solitude of himself outside of panoptican/outside of synoptican/outside of enlightenment/ outside of his/story/outside of the cold and cruel world/him a K9 canine/ innocent mammal/noble savage/

CANON FIRE IS A BLIND INSTITUTION

Reifications of blue sky people injected into the veins of my plasma screen/ The taxonomy begins with stereotypes of the tragic mulatto morphing into the coonery of her mammies smile/One drop too dark for the ripples of her own signification/the post traumatic syndrome of her slavery resides in the gangsters paradise of a new media/of a new screen culture of disinformation/ Where the 4x4s of their lyrics is a false consciousness/Trick bags of style over content steering me away from curiosity/Steering me away from these books/Into the matrix of a directors cut/i am groomed and remade in the silhouettes of a one dimensional man/Seduced by the shimmering effects of baking foil/Windows of escapism hidden in a rock crystal/The crack fiend of her broken womb is an abused childhood of under aged sex workers and radical pole dancing/Alcoholism the language of her curses/Knife fighting the colour of her rage/Barbed wire the texture of her lovemaking/She who is pimpnotized by the seductive lure of pixel screens/game boys and game girls in a vicious game of head hunting/Simulacrums of reality/Broken off/ Amputated from the real of ether/i pause in the hope that i am far too crazy to go insane/i pause in the hope that the Godfather of this philosophunk will suddenly step forward and take me to the bridge/break it down like a Lindy Hopper popping off in a spasmodic moment of hip hop fantasm/ so i can jump off/ into the baptism of dead suicide notes/poems from the flies of stench and greed/the chalked outlines of their insect bodies smelling of formaldehyde/is this really art or just another Damien Hirsts' take on things?/The selective genius of their canon fire is a blind institution/An art for art sake politics of occupation/My belly full of ideas and yet i am hungry for revolution/the messengers feet is warm against my lips/The freshness of our blood is the coded verse of an hermetic text/His is an ancient wisdom blown from the future/predictions of Malcolm/Martin/Medgar/murdered/ Tragedy is the sorrow of a perditious angel/fallen/Broken into fragments of blue melancholy/ History is much more than the little folks of a grand narrative/Much more than Baraka/Kaufman/Joans/Breton/Much more than a poet/Much more than poems/Much more than the sum of itself/ Beyond food stamps/Beyond the heights of food mountains/Beyond the text/outside of it all/Ostracised/ignored/

APB

In words I discovered other words
Fell into a pool of language

Fell into other worlds

Became film
Screened
Screamed
Scripted
Con-scripted

Became fiction
Am fiction
Am fictionalised
Am fi-i-ig leaf
Am fig leaf
Hiding cock and woman part

Became diction
Addiction
Addicted
A DICTIONARY

Looked in dictionary
And became words again
Inky black page symbols pregnant with meaning

Became narrative
Became verse
Became versatile
Became me
        Me subject
        You Queen
Me subject
        You King
        King-dumb
        Dumb King
        Dumb Queen
        Queen-Dumb
Queendom rules the waves
Queendom rules over her subjects

Me not subject
Me object
Me object to cruelty
Me object to oppression
Me ob-jec-ti-fied
Me lionised
Me HUNTED
Me HAUNTED
Me HARRASSED

ME-ME-ME-ME SOCIETY
ME-so-ci-ety
DO-RAY-MI-FA-SO-LA-TI-DO
Me musical
Me experimental
Me mental
Me mentally insane
WIERD
Me scared
Me not liked very much
Me institutionalised
Me demonised
Me victimised

> Me off the wall
> Me fall off the wall
> Hurt head and break
> Me broken into pieces of misrepresentations
> Me the subject of rumour and idle gossip

Fragments of my postmodern self
Pastiched
Me and Humpty Dumpty can never be fixed
ME AND HUMPTY DUMPTY IN NEED OF A FIX
In need of stability
In need of a poem
Calling all poets
THIS IS AN APB
This is an all points bulletin
CALLING ALL THE KINGS HORSES AND ALL THE KINGS MEN
WHO ARE DOWN WITH PATRIARCH –key-key-key-keyz
To unlock the cage of women folk.

Solitary Fox Scene II

I see it
through the branches of a cancerous tree
its elongated shadow abstract as a blade upon the scorched earth policy of exanimate grass land
it moving like a wounded soldier through the coffin malls of commodity fetishism
it tiptoeing upon the putrid bank of a diseased canal
where the sunlight is aged and pale as junkies
where the stench of garbage lives amongst the politricks of truth and religion
where the pallbearer's song is an ode to the crack dealer's endz*
IT
you cunning fur-coated vixen thing
marvellous artwork penned with her fingers
out-foxing the sprawl
out-foxing the heat
woebegone
urban desert land.

Mud

In my chest there is a pain which isn't really a pain
Not even a sign of my imminent death
But a bird trying to get out
And she is the free spirit of my soul
And she is nature bound
In sync with the one-1
With the I
With the I-higher one-1
Equilibriumised

Her balance is my balance
And we are the roots of tomorrow songs
And we are the talk of long flower stems
And we are the sun and a peaceful moon alone in the mystery of it all
Earth man and woman child
Mud
Clay and water
The potter begins
Kinetic and craft-wheel magik
Ingenious fingers shaping womanity into curves
Her female guitar strings
Cast in the bone of reciprocal image makers

And for me her gift is a phallus
Must I remain incomplete?
Spoilt by the beauty of provocative women
My ~~need~~ greed my downfall
Industrial aged folk
Take-me-nology ~~take-me-knowledgee~~
Tech/no/logy?
The destruction of cars is the destruction of me.

BRIO-FYTE

I key the engine and start the beast/capitalisms social mobility capsule is the high of all highs/All this power between my legs/eye candy metal pods of speed and egotism/sexualised body parts in homage to ford/his cyborg time of day is a cocaine production line sexing mirrors/her nose a womb/ her womb a home where metal babies live/the fascist cries of their piston noise in need of breast oil and grease milk/she the erotic sperm whale of petrol stations/unlock her engine part and pour gas into it/erect steel of my trembling hand will force her open/she my Audi Locus table top dancer/ she my Corvette Stingray street walker/love me bitch/press on gas and turn to bullet speed/the funked up whore of cum stain liquid is a blur/ outside/beyond retina/beyond electrical impulse and optic nerve endings/ beyond photosensitive ganglion cells/beyond retino-hypothalamic tract/ suprachiasmatic nuclei/the expressionist landscape is a fast forward vision/ the dusty chalk line of trees and vertebrates is a smeared rendition of a circle in motion/reality in negotiation with itself/the eyes of my portholes are light eaters/I eat light in order to see light/i am the lighthouse keeper/a simple star in the complexity of planets/a simple planet in the complexity of stars/either way i am nature bound and holy/nose at the ready/my knives drawn/sitting on the lonesome highway of a country song/trying to distinguish between/ the smell of concrete and grass/

Perpendicularities in Fetishes of Rubber and Brass

Burnt embers of steam tainted with its own guilt/upward and rising like a flame in the phoenix of conscious women/silhouettes in the holes of impossible songs/the pain of your beauty is an opaque melancholy/a rude outline of some womanist fiction inscribed upon the lips of indomitable fountain pens/your flesh/a textwork quilt in polysemic skin tones of a Spanish guitar/protruding from the hips like a curvaceous outer flow of gendered body parts/scalpel blades of a dark invention/conjuring cyber whores/the provocative yoga positions of their collective spirit is a sexed up maths formula/perpendicularities in fetishes of rubber and brass/their fingers smelling of religion/the liquid orgasm of an enriched tongue food sliding in the up-stream of men/where water appears in the guise of rain fall/neo-expressionisms of spheric glass capsules/the textured clouds of their invention tasting like candyfloss/brush strokes of a complex illusion/the conjurer's magic in free fall/the conjurer's magic in free verse/the conjurer's magic set free/the end of narrative/and all that is broken can be moulded into new abstractions/made proper and fixed again/like the sticks and stones of a woman's heart beat/the broken embers of a life in drag/and what a drag this life of skin clothes/prosperity and makeup/neurotic lip pencils shaped like a penis/her mouth a cave in the fascism of his sex drive/war and beauty collide as le mouvement feminine explodes like a Barbie doll's implant/everywhere tits and arse speaking in an ad campaign/everywhere plastic/fake hair of man-made fibres trembling like a vibrator in the osculums of the pornographers lens/profiles of a rare snake bite/species of wrath/her venom/the spitefulness of barbed wire twisted into the curse of her servitude/

Poem for Ani-Difranco

The perpetual rhythm of everything
Night after night
Day after day
Of an endless wash cycle
Clothes upon clothes of baptism
Drowning in faith

Too much religion in the world
Too many poets
Art for art sake dross of solipsism
Genius mind of skilful fingers
Birth meaningful songs from your womb
From the cave of your guitar lung
Wooden sound chamber heaven
Smelling like a woman

The revolution is a girl
A twelve year old Peruvian sex worker
War is so bloody
And men are not just cruel to themselves.

Her ankhles on a slipperless shoe/version I-one

A group sex experimentation

The radical poets are without work and home/reality has won/tricked the living and poured their youth into pension schemes/the women have covered their beauty with makeup/piles and piles of even more illusion/the beauty of their looks becoming myth/thinking they can hide their tears in handkerchiefs/thinking they can straighten their curves with bendy spoons/ with hot metal spoons heated on the backs of turtle shells/androgyny their will to freedom and equality/the sexual revolution reduced to a pill/reduced to a poet/her weapons/her words/without stone to sharpen/defunct and workless/she spins like table tops in search of clothes/in search of something more than his gaze/his amputated fingers all over her body parts/all over her poems/he is in her hair/entering her freckles with the oversized shoes of an erect footprint/his presence/a thousand mouse droppings of some countries invasion/armies of himself looking for a fix/looking for a fit/she who is freaky can have the glass slipper/ be home around midnight/with tales of one/ two/ three in a bed of crinkled sheets/of pillow cases burning lawn crosses/strange fruit smells stinking of smoked afro-wigs/picnic baskets in black man pickle/marinated negro features/melanin paste mixed into war paintings/like cave symbols sewn onto stone/pressed into bone/the skin colourful tones of her poems radicalized/her switchblade-lashes cutting glances out of sugar paper/carving silhouettes into her/outside the black-footed rain is wounded/falls upon concrete and bleeds water stains/the salted tears of impersonated sorrow songs/the swans flight is a noir sheeted flow of spontaneous speech acts/iambic combustions of gay morphemes in an haute couture of stanza patterns/a marvellous display of showing off/in words of lace and frock closets/her dog-collar truths untold/confession over/

Her ankhles on a slipperless shu/ version II-2

4 Knee-O-su-ree-a-list powetz and Post-mow-dern academiks

Tha radikal powets R r without werk ande home/reel-al-i-ty haz w1 /chrickt tha liv-ing & poured theyre yuuth in 2 pen=shion skeemes/tha wu-men haave koverd thayre byooty with mayke-up^/piles and piles of eevan more illuuzion/tha byooty ov thayre looks B-cum-in mith/thin-king thay Kan hyde thayre tayrzes in hnd-ker-cheefs/thin-king thay Kan strayten thayre curves with bendi spoons/with hot metal spooonz heeted on tha baks of tertle shells/an-dro-jiny thayre will 2 free√dum and eqwaLitee/tha se-X-shoo-al revalooztion ree-doosed 2A pill/ree-doosed 2A powit /heyr wepuns/heyr werdz/with-Δ-owt stowne 2 shaarpen/deefunkct & werkless/s/he spinz lyke tayble to♥ps in sertch of clozes/in sertch of sum-thing more thahn hiz gayze/ hiz am-pyoo-tated fin-gerz all o☼ver her bod-e parts/all ov☼er her powimz/ hee iz in→ her hair/Ntering her freklz with tha O-vr-sized shooze of an Ereckt fut-pri-nt/his prey♥zense/a thowzand mowse jjroppings of some count☻ries in-vayzion/Rmeez of him-cself looking for A fix/looking for a fit/sheee whoo is freeeecky Kan have tha gl-ass slipper/ B howme around◙ mid-nite/with taylze of 1one/ 2two/ 3three in a bed of crin-kirled sheetz/ of pill-O Kases burning lawn ††††crosses/stray-nje froot smellz stinking of smowked afro-wigs/piknik bar-sketz in blk m☻ ☻ ☻ ☻an pickle/marinated ne☻ ☺ ☻gro feet-churz/melanin pay-ste mixed into war payn-tingz/like cay-ve simblz sown onto stowne/pressed into bowne/the skin cu-ler-ful tones of her powims radiKalized/her switchblade-lashes cutting glances out of shoogar payper/car-v-ing sil-how-ettes into eeeether/owt-c-ide thah bl☻ ☻ ☻ ☻ak-footed rayne is wooondid/fawlls ↑↑↑↑↑up↑on concreet and bleedz water staynz/thah sawl-ted teerz of imper-sow-nait-ed so-rroe songz/ the swanz fly-t is a noir sheeted floe of spon-tay-nee-us speech aKts/i-am-bik com-bus-tee-onz of g-ay morpheemz in an awt coo-chture of stanza patt-ernz/a mar-v-lus diz-playe of showin off/in werdz of layse and frok clozets/ her dog-Kollar trooths un-towld/con-fe-tion O-ver/

CIRCLES OF POLYSEMY

Dear Poets & friends
I speak to you in verse
Because truth is subjective
Your decoding is another encoding
& so it seems
  We go around
In circles of polysemy
Each to their own patois
Sucking on our own tongues
Trying to understand
The meaning of life
Trying to grab a hold
Of what isn't really there

We are neither fixed
Or unfixed
By love
Chains
Or racial codes

But out there
On the in-between of things

Where the lies unfold
And poetry hurts

Poem That Gets Up Nose & Into Arse-Crack Phunke

Black Poststructuralism 4 Bank Managers and London Cab Drivers

---

how i dig writin'
crazee powim stuff
tht getz unda skin
and fin-ger-nayle
↑up nowse and into arse-crak phunke

burr-o-win' deep
in-2 ware cayvez live
throo doorz
in-2 warrenz
in-2 house
lost in theez labi-rin-thyne twists and terns

deep
deep
deep-I-go

in-2 her sex juices/
in-2 her sex drivin' moanz lik/e Wynton's trum-pet-Ed black star☼-liner townz of
jah rastafari blazin fire pon-de bald headz

bt deeper stilL
in-2 the bus-ted vaynz of a john coltrane solow
wayre the dark deep owsh-anz
R black♠
& strong (currents)

miss-tee-ree-US
mer-Q-ree-AL &
straynge

cree-chures of sum ra-dee-kal ar(k)t work

ima-gi-nazion
so strong
ni-ther he-van
nor hell can ree-zide there

ima-gi-nazion
so strong
real-I-jhon kan't cum-peet.